Earth

by Henry Pluckrose

Gareth Stevens Publishing
A WORLD ALMANAC EDUCATION GROUP COMPANY

Please visit our web site at: www.garethstevens.com
For a free color catalog describing Gareth Stevens' list of high-quality books
and multimedia programs, call 1-800-542-2595 (USA) or 1-800-461-9120 (Canada).
Gareth Stevens Publishing's Fax: (414) 332-3567.

Library of Congress Cataloging-in-Publication Data

Pluckrose, Henry Arthur.
    Earth / by Henry Pluckrose. — North American ed.
        p. cm. — (Let's explore)
    Includes bibliographical references and index.
    ISBN 0-8368-2960-3 (lib. bdg.)
    1. Geology—Juvenile literature.   2. Earth—Juvenile literature.
    [1. Geology.   2. Earth.]   I. Title.
    QE29.P65   2001
    550—dc21   2001031113

This North American edition first published in 2001 by
Gareth Stevens Publishing
A World Almanac Education Group Company
330 West Olive Street, Suite 100
Milwaukee, WI 53212 USA

This U.S. edition © 2001 by Gareth Stevens, Inc. Original edition © 2000 by Franklin Watts.
First published in 2000 by Franklin Watts, 96 Leonard Street, London, EC2A 4XD, United
Kingdom. Additional end matter © 2001 by Gareth Stevens, Inc.

Series editor: Louise John
Series designer: Jason Anscomb
Gareth Stevens editor: Monica Rausch
Gareth Stevens designer: Katherine A. Kroll

Picture credits: Bruce Coleman – cover, pp. 6 (Pacific Stock), 12 (Dr. Eckart Pott),
14 (William S. Paton), 18, 23 (Peter Terry), 20 (Bruce Coleman Ltd.), 24 (Dr. Stephen Coyne);
Impact p. 11 (Jonathan Pimlott); Planet Earth Pictures p. 17 (Steve Bloom); Oxford Scientific
Films p. 27 (Steve Littlewood); Robert Harding p. 31 (Geoff Renner); Still Pictures p. 15
(Delpho); Images Colour Library p. 28; Tony Stone Images p. 9 and title page (Kerrick James);
PhotoDisc Volumes: Spacescapes p. 4.

Printed in the United States of America

1 2 3 4 5 6 7 8 9 05 04 03 02 01

Contents

As you are reading this book, you are moving very quickly around the Sun on a huge ball of rock. This ball of rock is our planet — Earth.

Earth is made up of layers of rock. The outer layers of rock are hard and cold. The inner layers are hot. Some inner layers are so hot that the rock is liquid, like the red-hot rock flowing out of this volcano.

Rocks on the surface of Earth are worn down by wind and rain. They also are smoothed by water running in streams and rivers, and they are cracked by ice and frost.

Over many years, Earth's rocks have been breaking into tiny pieces. Some of the pieces are so small you can crumble them between your fingers.

Tiny pieces of rock sometimes mix with tiny pieces of dead plants and animals to form soil. Plants, such as flowers and trees, need soil to grow.

Soil also provides a home for
many different animals.

Worms, moles, and some rabbits
live underground in the soil.

When soil gets wet, it becomes sticky mud. Some animals, such as elephants, cover themselves with mud to keep cool. Can you think of another animal that likes to cover itself with mud?

We can find many different types of soil and rock both on and inside Earth. We dig rocks out of Earth in places called quarries.

Granite is a very hard rock. It
is a good rock for building walls
because it does not wear out.

Marble is another hard rock. Marble is usually one color with streaks of another color, such as gray or white, running through it. Artists often use this beautiful rock to make statues.

Clay is a type of soil that is very soft and sticky. It can be molded into different shapes. After we shape clay, we can bake it in a hot oven to make it hard. We can use clay to make bricks, tiles, and dishes. What is this man making out of clay?

These cliffs are made of chalk. Chalk is soft, crumbly rock that has many uses. It is used to make cement for sidewalks. Farmers use chalk in the fertilizers they put on their fields to help crops grow. How do you use chalk?

This oil rig is pumping oil out from under the seafloor. Oil, coal, and gas come from below Earth's surface. They are called fossil fuels. We use these fuels to heat our houses and to run machines.

Earth gives us everything we need: soil to grow crops for food; rocks to build houses and buildings; and oil, coal, and gas to run machines. We must take care of our beautiful Earth!

Index

More Books to Read

Fuel. Let's Investigate (series). Catherine J. Bernardy
     (Creative Education)

How to Dig a Hole to the Other Side of the World.
     Faith McNulty (HarperTrophy)

Look Inside the Earth. Poke and Look (series). Gina Ingoglia
     (Grosset and Dunlap)